CALLED TO CARE

WORKBOOK

A Companion Guide to
Called To Care:
Ministering to Special Populations Within
our Communities and Churches.

Dr. Patricia Lott

Called to Care Workbook:
Ministering to Special Populations within Our Churches
Copyright @ 2015 Shacklebuster Ministries

All Scripture Quotations unless otherwise stated are taken from
the King James Version of the Bible

Requests for workshops / information should be addressed to:
Dr. Patricia Lott
Shacklebuster Ministries
schacklebusterconference@yahoo.com

ISBN: 978-0-9827592-3-3

Printed in the United States of America

Psalm 139:23 & 24 says "Search me, O God, and know my heart: try me, and know my thoughts: And see if there be any wicked way in me, and lead me in the way everlasting. Psalm 26:2 says "Examine me, O Lord, and prove me; try my reins and my heart."

You have just begun a journey of self-discovery. I know that when you signed up for this workshop or purchased the book Called to Care you have very altruistic thoughts in your heart and mind. You have sat on the pew in your church and on the porch of your community and you have seen so much need, hurt and tears. You have wondered many times and cried out to God many times for help and received the answer, "That's why I showed you. So that you can help" You feel powerless. You just don't know what to say or how to say it and you fear saying or doing the wrong thing. Then you saw the book or signed up for the workshop and you thought, "Finally, a tool to help me answer the call to care."

Well, if you have been reading the book or listening to the facilitator you are finding yourself squirming in your chair and shaking in your boots. Little did you realize that before you could actually do this thing you have to, in the words of Paul, *2 Corinthians 13:5 "Examine yourselves, whether ye be in the faith; prove your own selves. Know ye not your own selves, how that Jesus Christ is in you, except ye be reprobates?"* You are finding so much of this information is making you uncomfortable or causing you to feel some kind of something, but you are determined to help.

This workbook which is a companion journal to the book Called to Care is where you are going to place your concerns, shortcomings, questions and prayers as you travel along this journey. 2 Timothy 2:21 says, "If a man therefore purge himself from these, he shall be a vessel unto honour, sanctified, and **meet** for the master's **use**, and prepared unto every good work." This is why the exercises are designed to help reinforce the information that you have been given and help you gain comfort in taking it from the page to the life.

I know that you are going to do just fine and that you will come out of this a force to be reckoned with as you fill your "Call to Care" in your pews and communities. Your Pastors and neighbors are going to be so thankful that the Lord has sent you to be a help. Thank you for stopping long enough to see the bush that was on fire and yet did not burn, turning to see what and how it plays out in your life

Yours through the Blood of the Lamb

Dr. Patricia Lott

TABLE OF CONTENT

"Love and compassion are necessities, not luxuries. Without them humanity cannot survive."—Dalai Lama

~ Prayer of St. Francis of Assisi ~

Lord, make me an instrument of Thy peace;
Where there is hatred, let me sow love;
Where there is injury, pardon;
Where there is error, the truth;
Where there is doubt, the faith;
Where there is despair, hope;
Where there is darkness, light;
And where there is sadness, joy.

O Divine Master,
Grant that I may not so much seek
To be consoled, as to console;
To be understood, as to understand;
To be loved as to love.

For it is in giving that we receive;
It is in pardoning that we are pardoned;
And it is in dying that we are born to eternal life. Amen.

~Amen~

~ Before Care ~

"Prepare thy work without, and make it fit for thyself in the field; and afterwards build thine house."
Pr 24:27

~ Working and Walking it Out ~

1. Take an inventory of yourself. After reading the introduction and chapter on Before-Care.

   - What are some mindsets or behaviors that are hindering you from seeing the bush that burneth but is not consumed?

   _____

   _____

   _____

   _____

   _____

   _____

   - What are some things that you can implement right now so that you can see the needs in your congregation and community?

   _____

   _____

   _____

   _____

   _____

   _____

   _____

- What is your greatest fear in actually stepping out of your comfort zone to actually meet a need?

_____

_____

_____

_____

_____

_____

- What is a challenge that you are taking to the Lord to help you overcome?

_____

_____

_____

_____

_____

_____

2. For the next three days SEE what is in your congregation and community. Do not make contact and try to see if you can do this. Just do like Moses and turn aside and see this great sight. What did you notice that you really hadn't actually SEEN before:

Day 1: _____

_____

_____

_____

_____

_____

Day 2_____

_____

_____

_____

_____

_____

Day 3: _____

_____

_____

_____

_____

_____

~*Journal*~

What was this exercise like for you? What did you feel? What did you see? What did you learn about yourself and your perceptions and biases?

_____

_____

_____

_____

_____

_____

_____

_____

_____

_____

_____

_____

_____

_____

_____

_____

_____

_____

~ Prayer ~

Father I come to you today thanking you for awakening me to the needs that are around me. For those who sit in worship with me, empower me at the appropriate time to demonstrate the care compassionately that they need. For those in my community, the teacher, the technician, the plumber, the construction worker, the homeless, helpless and infirmed that I see every day, it is my prayer that you find me ready and worthy to schedule a mission encounter that I may manifest your love to them.

-Amen

Remember to come back to this page and date it each time you feel the Lord answering this prayer.

~ GRIEF AND LOSS ~

"Thus saith the LORD; A voice was heard in Ramah, lamentation, and bitter weeping; Rahel weeping for her children refused to be comforted for her children, because they were not." Jeremiah 31:15

~ Working and Walking it Out ~

Below you will find twenty statements. Place a "Y" next to a statement that would be compassionate and effective with a grieving spouse or parent. Place an "N" next to those that would not.

_____ I am so sorry for your loss.

_____ I wish I had the right words, just know I care.

_____ At least she lived a long life, many people die young.

_____ There is a reason for everything.

_____ Be strong.

_____ I don't know how you feel, but I am here to help in any way I can.

_____ You and your loved one will be in my thoughts and prayers.

_____ My favorite memory of your loved one is….

_____ Aren't you over him yet, he has been dead for a while now.

_____ You can have another child still.

_____ I am always just a phone call away.

_____ He is in a better place.

_____ Give a hug instead of saying something.

_____ She brought this on herself.

_____ She did what she came here to do and it was her time to go.

_____ She was such a good person God wanted her to be with him.

_____ We all need help at times like this, I am here for you.

_____ I am usually up early or late, if you need anything.

_____ Saying nothing, just be with the person.

_____ I know how you feel.

~ Journal~

Talk about your experience in this chapter. What did you feel? What did you learn about yourself and your perceptions and biases? What has changed?

_____

_____

_____

_____

_____

_____

_____

_____

_____

_____

_____

_____

_____

_____

_____

_____

_____

_____

_____

~ **Prayer** ~

Father I come to you today asking for your strength as I listen to and help those who have experienced so great a loss. Help me to not take what they are going through lightly but to be the solid shoulder and understanding ear that even if it is without words and just my presence can be used by you to help them to make it through
-Amen

Remember to come back to this page and date it each time you feel the Lord answering this prayer.

~ DIVORCE ~

"…but God hath called us to peace" 1 Corinthians 7:15

~ *Working and Walking it Out* ~

Looking at the three scenarios below, choose the one which is the most challenging for you to minister to: Divorcee' Leaving Spouse or Child of Divorce. Document how you would respond, as well as how you want to be able to respond.

(A) Divorcee': You have noticed someone in the congregation in the "Naked Divorce Grieving Cycle" Open up a conversation with them using what you have learned to comfort and help them.

(B) Leaving Spouse: You are the chairperson of a banquet that normally both partners would attend. The leaving spouse asks you the particulars (time, place, cost, speaker, if you need any help) Have a conversation with them.

(C) You notice the withdrawn child of recently divorced parents. Normally they are bubbly and full of life. Today they are withdrawn and in tears. They want to see their daddy. They feel as if they are betraying mommy for wanting to see daddy. They say to you that they are a bad little child because if they had been good, daddy would not have left. Spend time ministering to this child.

~Journal~

There was a lot of information to sift through in this chapter. Some of it may have been hard to read and find compassion for. Talk about it here. Be sure to ask the Lord in Prayer to help you to soften your heart and be effective in helping those in your congregations and communities to heal.

_____

_____

_____

_____

_____

_____

_____

_____

_____

_____

_____

_____

_____

_____

_____

_____

~ Prayer ~

Father I come to you today realizing that it is more likely than not that I may encounter the carnage of dissolved marriages in my corner of the world. Prick my heart so that this is not an easily accepted and overlooked trauma simply because it is normal for society in these days. Give me the words to say and the heart to hear those I come in contact with who have found themselves divorced. Give me a kind heart and understanding heart to respect and help to recover the one who felt that there was no other way than to walk away from their marriage. Lastly Lord I ask for a heart full of love and action to help the children of divorce.

-Amen

Remember to come back to this page and date it each time you feel the Lord answering this prayer.

~ *FAMILIES OF PRISONERS* ~

"But Mary Kept these things and Pondered them in her heart" Lk 2:19

~ *Working and Walking it Out* ~

Think about your congregation and your community. What types of ministry is in place for the family members of prisoners?

Develop a support group for the following three populations: A) spouses, B) children of prisoners and 3) adolescent children of prisoners, in your church. Who knows maybe a ministry for your church will be birthed out today.

_____

_____

_____

_____

_____

_____

_____

_____

_____

_____

_____

_____

_____

_____

_____

_____

_____

_____

_____

_____

_____

_____

_____

_____

_____

_____

_____

_____

_____

_____

_____

_____

_____

_____

_____

_____

_____

~Journal~

There has been a lot to think about in this chapter. Write your challenges, questions and concerns here to lay before the Lord.

_____

_____

_____

_____

_____

_____

_____

_____

_____

_____

_____

_____

_____

_____

~ **Prayer** ~

Father please forgive me. I have thought many times about ways in which to minister to and help those who have found themselves incarcerated but I find that I have not given much thought to those loved ones left behind to deal with the fallout. I thank you for opening my awareness and bring forth from me a compassionate ministry for all in this special population that you form a mission encounter with me.

-Amen

~ GLBTQ COMMUNITY ~

"The LORD hath appeared of old unto me, saying, Yea, I have loved thee with an everlasting love: therefore with lovingkindness have I drawn thee" Jeremiah 31:3

~ Working and Walking it Out ~

I want for you to write down some things that you can do with each section of this population in your church in order to create a safe place and safe environment within yourself so that you can be used by God to help bring deliverance.

_____

_____

_____

_____

_____

_____

_____

_____

_____

_____

_____

_____

_____

_____

~ Journal~

Write down the biases that you discovered in yourself when it comes to this population. Next write down ways in which you have been unfeeling and uncaring in your conversations and perceptions. Repent of these things before the Lord. He is waiting to heal so that you can help to heal.

_____

_____

_____

_____

_____

_____

_____

_____

_____

_____

_____

_____

_____

_____

_____

_____

~ Prayer ~

Father You see my confessed shortcomings with these people that you have created and loved with an everlasting love. I am so sorry for my ignorance and my hatred and my misunderstanding and my fears. I am sorry for the way I have pushed away and driven instead of nurtured and drawn and I ask for your divine forgiveness. I am asking you Lord to use me to be an instrument of peace and a light illuminating your love. Help me to be a bridge to carry them over to you.

-Amen

Remember to come back to this page and date it each time you feel the Lord answering this prayer.

~ P K'S ~

"Therefore all things whatsoever ye would that men should do to you, do ye even so to them..." Matthew 7:12

~ Working and Walking it Out ~

For the next 4 weeks make an effort to love on your PKs using the Do's and Don'ts in Called to Care as a springboard if you can't think of a starting point. Report in your journal the changes that you see in them...in yourself. It may be that this is the beginning of a beautiful much needed relationship.

Wk, 1 _____

_____

_____

_____

Wk. 2 _____

_____

_____

_____

Wk.3 _____

_____

_____

_____

Wk. 4 _____

_____

_____

_____

~Journal~

Honestly discuss your attitude, opinions and actions past or present toward your pastor's child(ren) or the pastor's children in your neighborhood. Repent of your bias if necessary. Seek forgiveness from them if need be.

_____

_____

_____

_____

_____

_____

_____

_____

_____

_____

_____

_____

_____

_____

_____

_____

_____

_____

~ Prayer ~

God of all mercy comfort and peace, I am coming to you today because as I reflect on the Pastor's children I see how many times I criticized, superimposed my opinions and bias, held a double standard, took advantage of who their father was for my own personal need and just downright ignored them except for the times I had something negative to say to or about them. I ask that you forgive me my error. Lord as I move toward reconciliation and restoration word my mouth, lead me as to how to bring them close to my heart and teach them intercession, love, compassion and understanding. Help me to weigh out my timing and expectations of their father realizing that some things really can wait and realizing that I while I am only one member of the church that if every member calls 1 time we have deprived children of their father for a full day so that my one time of seeking the Lord, waiting until appropriate times can make a world of difference to his children. Use me as a light and an example to the other parishioners of how to take the Pastor's children into consideration. After all, much like my own children, he will only have them in the home to raise and interact daily with them for a short period of time. With humility I submit this prayer

-Amen

~ MEMBERS WHO HAVE CHILDREN WITH DISABILITIES ~

*"But Jesus said, Suffer little children, and **forbid them not**, to come unto me: for of such is the kingdom of heaven." Matthew 19:14*

~ Working and Walking it Out ~

Create a compassionate care workshop for your ministry to demonstrate ways in which to help the parents of children with special needs. What would you enclose, how would you go about it? Pray and see if the Lord wants for you to bring awareness to your local assembly, speak to the Pastor about it.

~Journal~

Work through the following three questions after reading the corresponding chapter in Called to Care. Do this while you are still raw and have not had time to rationalize or justify your feelings

1) What emotions did I experience as I read the words of Sonya this chapter?

_____

_____

_____

_____

_____

_____

2) Reading trough this chapter, what things did I learn / discern that Parents with special needs may need from me by way of help? (ex to watch the child during service so that they can get the most out of their time of worship)

_____

_____

_____

_____

_____

3) When reviewing Adrianne's list of what and what not to say I learned?

~ Prayer ~

Father please forgive me. So many times I have been short tempered and harbored ill feelings toward those who have children with disabilities. I find that in my zeal to worship I have negated the fact that these parents want to worship as well. I have come to realize that as much as I want for you to receive my worship, in like manner I need to be tolerant as you receive their worship. Who am I to tell someone how to worship simply because they have special needs? Father I have come to realize that with no maliciousness of heart and mind I have often times said things that were offensive. I am asking you now to word my mouth and give me newness of actions and thought as I strive to be a help and not be a stumbling block to those in my community and church who have special needs or are the parents of children with special needs.

-Amen

Remember to come back to this page and date it each time you feel the Lord answering this prayer.

~ ADDICTIONS & RECOVERY~

"When Jesus heard it, he saith unto them, They that are whole have no need of the physician, but they that are sick: I came not to call the righteous, but sinners to repentance." Mark 2:17

"… And Jesus said unto her, Neither do I condemn thee: go, and sin no more" John 8:11

~ *Working and Walking it Out* ~

Read the Exercise below and respond to the questions at the end in to see how much your understanding of the disease of addiction has grown.

Ted's and Jane's Big Adventure

Ted and Jane graduated from high school in May. Both planned to go to State University in the fall. Ted is diabetic and on insulin. Jane is chemically dependent and is involved in a local AA group for young adults.

Ted found out he was diabetic when he passed out at a soccer match in his freshman year and was taken to the hospital. Jane admitted she had a drinking problem during her sophomore year when she passed out at a party and then wrecked her car later that night on the way home. Both were hospitalized at City Hospital. Ted spent 8 days in the Endocrine Unit and attended daily classes for diabetics. Jane was a patient in the Substance Abuse Unit for 28 days and attended group and lectures every day.

Although Ted and Jane didn't know each other very well, both were invited to a Fourth of July party given by Buz, a mutual friend. His parents own a lake house on Clear Water Lake. They also have a ski boat and a swimming dock. Buz's parents were in Europe for the summer. Jane and Ted were fired up for the party! The girls were instructed to bring the food; the boys were to bring the alcohol. Jane made her "to-die-for" double chocolate brownies. Ted got his older brother to buy some Ever Clear so that they could make a batch of Purple Passion.

The fourth of July turned out to be a perfect day: bright and hot. Everyone piled in their cars; a few put down their convertible tops, others opened their sunroofs, and everyone blasted their stereos. The trip to the lake took about an hour. On arriving, coolers, picnic baskets and swim bags were unloaded. Then everyone headed for the boat dock. The boat was on the first ski run of the day by 11:00 AM.

Ted, an avid water skier, had trouble waiting for his turn to take a run. He hung back for the sake of politeness but quickly got sick of watching others fly across the water. Finally, when most of the group was breaking for lunch, Ted had a chance to go out. As he fought with the tangled rope and clumsy skis in the water, it flashed across his mind that he had not done his blood test that morning and had completely forgotten to take his morning insulin. This fleeting realization was wiped away as the ski rope, now taut, pulled him forward. He responded automatically, positioned himself and yelled, "Hit it!" After a great run that lasted 20 minutes, Ted was picked up and on his way back to the dock. Eating, drinking, and merrymaking were the order of the day.

Jane, in the meantime, had been fighting the familiar war on the battlefield of her mind. Although none of her friends pushed alcohol in her direction, the fact that it was all around her was hard to take. She watched as her friends drank and laughed and seemed to be having so much more fun than she was.

Jane wanted to be a part of it all and decided that a couple of beers, after all of these months of abstinence, wouldn't hurt.

Ted began to feel weird and shaky. He thought it was because he'd had a long, hard ride on the water and he'd probably burned up all the calories of his breakfast -on-the-run. He figured he would be fine after he ate something. The dock was loaded with coolers and baskets of food - everything from fried chicken and chocolate cake to ham sandwiches and deviled eggs. Ted's thoughts raced, "I deserve a day off that stupid diet. For once I'm eating and drinking everything everyone else is!" Jane's double chocolate brownies were outstanding. An hour later, after eating a huge plate of forbidden food, Ted didn't feel very well. No one seemed to notice how strange he felt. He decided to go up to the cabin and...everything went black.

Ted's passing out seemed to put a lid on the party atmosphere. Several guys rushed him to City Hospital while the girls called his parents. "Some kind of diabetic crisis or coma," the doctor said.

Jane didn't want anything changing the high *she* was on. The "couple of beers" had become a six pack by the time the guys got back from the hospital. They reported that Ted has almost gone into a diabetic coma. The doctor said he was out of danger now and his parents were on their way. Everyone was relieved. Now it was time to let the party continue!

Mixing Purple Passion seemed a good way to jump-start a party atmosphere. Jane found a plastic dishpan under the kitchen sink. Someone brought grape Kool-Aid and Ted's Ever Clear was on the kitchen table. Five minutes later, the "brew" was mixed. Jane was aware of the sobering, rocketing buzz that caught her and carried her to that old familiar place of oblivion. At first she felt in the center of things as the music blasted and she joked and laughed with her friends. Later it was more like she was the observer watching herself from some distant place. What was she doing in the bedroom with Chuck? Maybe it really didn't matter - or did it? Some physical pull was in charge; she could only stumble along with it. She was aware of the weight of Chuck's body on hers, the smell of his hair, and a feeling of exposure, shame and then it all went black...

Questions

1. Who was responsible for Ted's diabetes? For Jane's alcoholism?

   _____

   _____

   _____

2. Who was responsible for Ted's coma? For Jane's blackout?

_____

_____

_____

3. Where did Ted go wrong?

_____

_____

_____

4. Where did Jane go wrong?

_____

_____

_____

5. How could Ted have managed his disease in this situation?

_____

_____

_____

6. How could Jane have managed her disease in this situation?

_____

_____

_____

Self -Reflection Questions

1. What new information did you learn from this story?

_____

_____

_____

2. How would you feel if Ted and Jane were members of your church or community?

_____

_____

_____

3. How would you feel if Jane were in your daughter or other family member?

_____

_____

_____

4. How would you feel if Ted were your son or other family member?

_____

_____

_____

5. Is it possible to "party" responsibly? (This question speaks to those whose reformation does not teach and preach caseation of worldly activities)

_____

_____

_____

~ Journal ~

This chapter I know, was a challenging read for you. So many times it is our own mindsets and lack of knowledge that hinder us from being able to help a person. Talk about the journey through this chapter in the journal space provided.

_____

_____

_____

_____

_____

_____

_____

_____

_____

_____

_____

_____

_____

_____

_____

_____

_____

~ Prayer ~

Lord God in heaven Creator of all things. You have all power to heal those who are struggling with the devastating disease of addiction. I pray God you would intercede in their lives and flood their eyes with light. So they can know and understand the hope to which You have called them. Give them strength and courage. Take away their fears, grief, anxieties, and resentments. Send your word, God, and heal them. Rescue them from the pit of destruction. Allow them to live and not die. Heal their broken hearts and bind up their wounds, curing all of their pains and sorrows. Allow them to hear your call, allow them the grace to never ever give up and to always stay focused on you... Fill their hearts with your word, for your word is life to all who find it and health for the whole body, mind, and spirit... Help me I pray that I will have discerning in this area and will be approved by you to help my brother or sister in the ministry of caring I pray these things in Jesus Holy Name

-Amen

Remember to come back to this page and date it each time you feel the Lord answering this prayer.

~ ABUSE IN THE HOUSE OF GOD ~

"In the same day also will I punish all those that leap on the threshold, which fill their masters' houses with violence and deceit" Zephaniah 1:9

~ *Working and Walking it Out* ~

Think about your neighborhood and your place of worship. What is in place to offer practical help for those who may be in an abusive situation? Make yourself a pocket booklet of scriptures that you can use when confronted with abuse.

1) Create an escape plan for someone in a domestic violence situation

_____

_____

_____

_____

_____

_____

_____

_____

_____

2) Create an activity that inspires confidentiality and comfort that can be used with children in an abusive situation that will get them to open up to you.

_____

_____

_____

_____

_____

_____

_____

_____

_____

_____

_____

_____

_____

_____

_____

_____

_____

_____

_____

3) create a comfort plan for the elderly who are in abusive situations that can be used to get them to open up to you so that you can begin to get them help.

_____

_____

_____

_____

_____

_____

_____

_____

_____

_____

_____

_____

_____

_____

_____

_____

_____

_____

4) Create a safe place that is compassionate yet structured enough to use with those who have suffered religious abuse. Lastly, journal concerning the scriptures that you learned in this chapter

_____

_____

_____

_____

_____

_____

_____

_____

_____

_____

_____

_____

_____

_____

_____

_____

_____

_____

~ Journal~

Journal concerning the scriptures that were reviewed in Called to Care concerning what the Bible says about each type of abuse.

_____

_____

_____

_____

_____

_____

_____

_____

_____

_____

_____

_____

_____

_____

_____

_____

~ Prayer ~

Dear Jesus, you have instructed us to weep with those who weep and mourn with those who mourn as well as rejoice with those who rejoice. I cannot understand what my sister and brother are going through in this abusive situation but I feel their hurt, their pain, their confusion and fear. I rebuke those spirits in the name of Jesus and I am asking you through your Spirit to use me as an instrument of peace, comfort and advocacy so that he/she can once again live in peace and safety

-Amen

Remember to come back to this page and date it each time you feel the Lord answering this prayer.

MY PERSONAL TOOLBOX

Throughout your journey with Called to Care you should have found that the Lord was speaking specific scripture to you for use in your mission encounters with the lost and hurting in your churches and communities. Take some time to jot them down complete with their address and the population with which you will use them. Remember, just because you have always heard this scripture in reference to one thing doesn't mean that the Lord is not going to use it with the population with which He has spoken to you. Also keep in mind that simply because a scripture addresses a specific population does not mean that this is one of the scriptures for your tool box.

_____

_____

_____

_____

_____

_____

_____

_____

_____

_____

_____

~ After Care ~

~Working and Walking it Out ~

Everyone needs someone. Yes it is true that the scriptures and prayer answer all things but think about it. Jesus Himself had Peter, James and John while in the Flesh. Out of those three he had a special closeness to John earning him the reputation of "The one whom Jesus loved." You have just spent time helping someone to heal. You have just emptied yourself of compassion. Undoubtedly you have heard some things and experienced some things and you do not know what to with those things. You feel the weight of the person whom has just been freed. Who can you turn to? Below list three (3) full wells as identified in Called to Care that you can confidently go to for your own emotional health.

1. _____
2. _____
3. _____

Now I want for you to list three things that you can do to de-stress

1. _____
2. _____
3. _____

Now list the three scriptures that bring you to a place of peace.

1. _____
2. _____
3. _____

~ Journal~

You have just finished attending the 5 day workshop, the weekend camp, or the 3 day intensive or reading the book Called to Care. I want to thank you for answering this call that so many have ignored in the society in which we live today. A society that is fearful of touching and connecting with one another in an endeavor to avoid hurt or backlash of various forms. I want to thank you for caring enough to act or as the scripture says "be moved with compassion." For our last journal entry, talk about your journey through this process. Where were you when we started? Where did you find yourself as we traveled through our journey? Where are you now that we have reached the end of our time together? How are you different? What have you been empowered and inspired to do?   May the Lord richly bless you for your act of love in service to His special population?

_____

_____

_____

_____

_____

_____

_____

_____

_____

_____

_____

_____

_____

_____

_____

_____

~ Prayer ~

The Full Original Copy of the Serenity Prayer
By

Reinhold Niebuhr (1892-1971)

God, give us grace to accept with serenity
the things that cannot be changed,
Courage to change the things
which should be changed,
and the Wisdom to distinguish
the one from the other.

Living one day at a time,
Enjoying one moment at a time,
Accepting hardship as a pathway to peace,
Taking, as Jesus did,
This sinful world as it is,
Not as I would have it,

Trusting that You will make all things right,
If I surrender to Your will,
So that I may be reasonably happy in this life,
And supremely happy with You forever in the next.

Amen.

www.ingramcontent.com/pod-product-compliance
Lightning Source LLC
Chambersburg PA
CBHW081231020426
42331CB00012B/3130